the Family of the Forgiven

Reidar A. Daehlin

Publishing House
St. Louis London

Concordia Publishing House, St. Louis, Mo.
Concordia Publishing House Ltd., London E. C. 1
Copyright © 1973 Concordia Publishing House
Library of Congress Catalog Card No. 72-96740
ISBN 0-570-03143-5

MANUFACTURED IN THE UNITED STATES OF AMERICA

To Marion

contents

Chapter One	SAY IT SO I CAN GRASP IT	11
Chapter Two	THE FAMILY OF THE FORGIVEN	16
Chapter Three	BORN, THEN WHAT?	27
Chapter Four	MY FATHER'S NAME— AND MINE	36
Chapter Five	FORGIVEN AND FORGIVING	46
Chapter Six	CARE FOR THE OTHERS	56
Chapter Seven	SURROGATE FATHER THE PRIEST IN YOUR HOUSE	67
Chapter Eight	A TRYST WITH THE MASTER	77

preface

During the past few years, as I have moved about the church and talked with many of our people in the congregations, I have become increasingly convinced that although there are countless fine theological books there is a need for a common man's picture of the Christian life and faith.

It must be a Biblical picture, but it must also be one with which the ordinary believer can identify, with which he can *feel* and which he can interpret more fully in the course of his everyday experiences, a framework that he can fill in and elaborate with the details of his daily life.

I believe the picture of "The Family of the Forgiven" meets this need. I have used it often in seminars, retreats, and family camps, also with youth groups in preaching, teaching, and conversation, and know that it catches on.

May this little volume be of help to the plain people of the church and to the many who struggle for certainty and hope for joy.

Chapter ONE

say it so I can grasp it

This is a mixed-up world. It is marked by a pervasive search for meaning and an intense hunger for belonging, but nevertheless it seems to specialize in confusion, uncertainty, and a sense of lostness. There has been so much written about the newness of the present age—its overwhelming expansion of knowledge, kaleidoscopic changes, vanishing mores and disappearing moorings, the pluralistic society, and the needs and characteristics of modern man—that it makes you dizzy.

In the midst of all this there has also been a barrage of analysis, condemnation, warning, and advice to the church's membership and the parish pastor, all the way from prophecy of doom and futility to a call for the quick discovery of new ideas, new images, new ways of saying the truth and expressing the faith. It has been said many times that we need to create an entirely new language and develop new thought forms if we are ever to communicate the Gospel to the present and future generations.

All this may be both needed and desirable, and much good may eventually come out of the turmoil, for the Holy Spirit is still at work. This we must believe. Nevertheless, much of today's theological writing is so complex, with such liberal coinage of terms, that it is often difficult to know exactly what is meant. Clarity is surely not characteristic of our times. Ordinary persons—and there are many of us—hunger for some simplicity, for something plain enough to grasp. "A word fitly spoken is like apples of gold in a setting of silver." (Prov. 25:11)

There is a need to say it so people can get hold of it, to use identifiable analogy that has some connection with available experience.

Is it not possible that the prospector in this new age may forget the "mother lode" in a frenzy of scratching at barren hills? Are we searching everywhere except where the treasure is most likely hidden? Should not the Scriptures yield the picture?

God has spoken to all generations through His Word. His message has caught the hearts and minds of people in many changing times. He whose view is eternal cannot have been so shortsighted as to limit His Word to the grasp of only a few fleeting generations. He has surely provided in the Bible the fitting imagery for each new and curent age.

The Bible speaks often in picture language. Many of its pictures were set in the framework of a time and society whose background and experience made it much easier to quickly get the message than it seems for us today. It takes a good deal of study for us in some instances to catch the vivid colors. Some come alive with a little transposing to modern terms and present-day idioms. Others are instantly applicable because they fit nicely even today.

Jesus, who was an exceptionally adept teacher, used picture language a great deal. One need only to read the parables to be struck by their powerful pictorial impact. We often do the same today. We paint a word picture to better express an idea. We use the expression "It is like . . . ." Ours is a visual age. When people feel they are not being heard they take to acting out their message, creating pictures. This is part of the reason for the new styles in dress and hair effected by the young in recent years. The Old Testament prophets sometimes used this kind of language to make a point.

Has God given us any special picture by which we may better understand His dealings with us and our relationship to Him? He has. What is there in the record of God's self-revelation that finds its counterpart in the modern scene, an identifiable analogy with experience common to our time? Let us take a careful look.

For us to know Him at all, even in small measure, God has chosen to come to us in human terms. He broke into human life in the person of Jesus Christ, His Son, and speaks to us in the Scriptures in human language and imagery. And He speaks through His Word today.

A number of years ago I began looking in the Bible for a particular, dominant "picture" by which to understand, at least in part, and to make my own God's way with His people and my life in Him.

Surely there are other pictures, but one that presses to the fore and which is threaded all the way through the Bible is the *Father-son* relationship, the imagery of the household, the picture of the family. It is rewarding to look for this as you read.

Here is something that still holds in our society, something that retains essential and recognizable features. It has a timelessness about it. This I can get hold of so that it becomes a part of me.

The picture of the believers as the household of God is thoroughly Biblical and understandable. It opens up the faith to plain people.

God is my Father, *our* Father. We are His family, with all that that entails.

Chapter TWO

the Family of the Forgiven

There has been a good deal of discussion lately about the church, the doctrine of the church, and the need for a clear definition. And yet we do define the church every time we confess our faith with the Apostles' Creed.

"I believe in the holy Christian [catholic] church, the communion of saints."

In this statement the comma indicates that the latter phrase explains the former. The Christian church *is* the communion of saints. But if the Christian church is the communion of saints, then it is of vital importance to know what a communion is, and to know who is a saint; otherwise the definition is of no use.

What is a "communion"?

Reduced to its simplest terms, a communion, and also community, is a group of people who share the same privileges and the same responsibilities. The *family* is the smallest and commonest example of a communion. So the communion of saints is the *family* of saints.

Now, who is a saint?

This word "saint" gives us more of a problem. There are many words which in the passage of time have had their meanings gradually altered or obscured through frequent misuse. The word saint is one of them. (Another example is the word "anxious," which is so regularly misused as a synonym for "eager" that in time it may have to officially take on that new meaning.)

A saint is usually thought of as someone who has achieved a behavior level much above the ordinary. An extra good person is sometimes called a saint. So people get to thinking primarily of the degree of moral and religious behavior of a person in using the word saint. But this is not the way the Scriptures use the word, nor is it the meaning it must carry in the Creed.

According to the Scriptures, *a saint is nothing more, and nothing less, than a forgiven person.* He is one who through faith in Jesus Christ as his personal Savior has craved, sought, received, and lives in the forgiveness of sin. This is a saint. *Every* forgiven believer is a saint. *Only* the forgiven are saints. I may be in need of a great deal of change and improvement in my life and yet be a saint. Conversely, I may have been a member of a church for decades, been extra busy with church work, taught a great many classes and racked up a beautiful record of benevolent conduct and still not be a saint, *if* through all this I have never come to the point of crying, "God, be merciful to me, the sinner!" A saint is simply a forgiven person, in Christ.

Therefore the Christian church is the family of the forgiven. It is the household of God, as Paul says so lucidly in Eph. 2:19-22: "So then you are no longer strangers and sojourners [tourists], but you are fellow citizens with the saints and members of the household of God, built upon the foundation of the apostles and prophets, Christ Jesus Himself being the cornerstone." (See also 1 Tim. 3:15)

This is your home. You *belong* here!

In thinking of this "family of the forgiven," this household of God, we begin with Him who calls it into being, who makes the family possible and gives it its character—"our Father."

God's early revelation of Himself, as given to the patriarchs, was as God Almighty. When He meets Moses in the early chapters of Exodus, His name is Jahweh, the Lord, He who *is.*

It isn't until the people of Israel have been rescued out of bondage by God's mighty hand, restored to the land of promise, and settled in it that the word *Father* becomes a part of His dealings with His redeemed people. When they are *home again*, He speaks as the Father.

I believe about the earliest use of this picture comes in 2 Sam. 7:14 and 1 Chron.17:13, where God speaks to David regarding his son Solomon, saying: "I will be his Father, and he shall be My son."

In Ps. 68:5 He is called the "Father of the fatherless," and Ps. 89:26 has, "Thou art my Father, my God."

The prophet Isaiah has two passages: one in Is. 9:6, where "Everlasting Father" is one of the titles of the Messiah, the coming One, and again in 63:16, "Thou, O Lord, art our Father, our Redeemer from of old is Thy name."

The picture of a yearning, loving, patient, and pleading Father, and also of a warning Father, as He deals with an errant people, occurs repeatedly in the Old Testament. "I taught Ephraim to walk," "You have been carried by Me from your birth," such expressions come again and again as God talks to His people.

In the prayer that Jesus taught us our communion with God is based on the initial words "Our Father." It is not just *my* Father, but *ours*. Jesus says: "Call no man your father on earth, for you have one Father, who is in heaven" (Matt. 23:9). The apostle Paul reemphasizes this in Eph. 4:6:

"One God and Father of us all." "I will be a father to you, and you shall be My sons and daughters" (2 Cor. 6:18). (See also Gal. 3:26-27)

Is there any better way for the human heart and mind to grasp the relationship between God and man than to see Him as the strong, wise, and loving Father, and ourselves as His beloved children?

Is there any better way to understand and experience our relationship to other people than in the framework of this same family picture? Here our joys and sorrows, defeats and triumphs assume their true meaning. Here the sharing, the support, the partnership, the hurts and the healing that make up the life of the family can be seen and known.

Now comes the big question: *How do I become a member of the family of the forgiven?*

This is where there is so much confusion. In spite of the clearest preaching on the way of salvation and the definite message of many hymns, it seems that people persist in thinking in terms of working for, earning, or meriting their place in God's family. We are often like a sick and poverty-stricken young man who first wants a list of the rules in the house to see if he can keep them before accepting the offer of adoption by someone who already loves him.

One night on a plane my seatmate poured out his troubles and expressed his desire to get right with God, but he kept coming back to the refrain: "I've got to try harder. I've got to change my ways first and do better in my life." It was not until he thought in terms of his own human birth that he found light and peace through the Scriptures we shared. But then he saw it and was glad.

Ask anyone, young or old: "How did you get into your own family?" The response is at first a puzzled look, until you press the point: "What did you have to do, to achieve, or accomplish before you got into your own human family? Was there some effort you had to make, some test you had to pass first?"

I have asked this both of groups and of individuals. Incidentally, for some reason the young respond more quickly than middle-aged or older people. Think about it for a while.

There can be only one answer: "Nothing! I did nothing. This life was given to me, totally. It is due entirely to the love of my parents. I was *born* into my family."

Any effort on the part of a baby during birth would be a hindrance and a danger rather than an asset, wouldn't it? Birth is something that is totally *given* out of love and accepted.

If we always kept this picture in mind, perhaps we wouldn't stray off into crediting ourselves with our salvation, but like beloved children would accept a good gift and live in it.

"Unless you turn and become like children, you will never enter the kingdom of heaven" (Matt. 18:3). It seems so difficult to keep this clear, and that of course pleases Satan.

Nicodemus, one of the elite in Israel, had the same problem. He came to Jesus one night, and during the conversation Jesus said: " 'Truly, truly, I say to you, unless one is born anew, he cannot see the kingdom of God.' Nicodemus said to Him, 'How can a man be born when he is old? Can he enter a second time into his mother's womb and be born?' Jesus answered, 'Truly, truly, I say to you, unless one is born of water and the Spirit, he cannot enter the kingdom of God. That which is born of the flesh is flesh, and that which is born of the Spirit is spirit' " (John 3:3-6). Jesus would not let him get lost in the mechanism of it. He used a picture to help Nicodemus see.

The Sacrament of Baptism is the point at which God takes us into His family and gives us new life. Sin estranged man from God's family. The forgiveness of sin removes the estrangement and gives a new life with God in Christ. Jesus by His life, death, and resurrection won this new life for us, making forgiveness full and free. When we are identified with Him in Baptism we are new creatures. "The old has passed away, behold, the new has come.

All this is from God, who through Christ reconciled us to Himself and gave us the ministry of reconciliation" (2 Cor. 5:17-18). God does it, and God gives it. No newborn babe bothers to try to figure out how his birth came about. The thing to do is to accept it, respond to it, and enjoy it.

I have gone back often to a thought brought out by a young pastor leading a group in devotions some years ago: "When did the prodigal son discover his sonship? Not until he discovered the forgiving father." Luther's Small Catechism puts it so plainly: "For where there is forgiveness of sin, there is life and salvation."

Accepting this action of God, gladly receiving His gift, is faith. "You have been saved through faith . . . it is the gift of God—not because of works, lest any man should boast." (Eph. 2:8-9)

When we think in terms of our birth as totally given and as the way in which we came into our families, and then go from there to the picture of birth by God's gift into his family, the family of the forgiven, some will have a new and disturbing question, because they were not *born* into their families.

We were in lively discussion of this point at a youth seminar some years ago when one of the young people, who had been silent for a while, spoke up: "What if you're adopted?"

A marvel of God's love is that he has taken care

of this too. Look at Gal. 4:4-7: "But when the time had fully come, God sent forth His Son, born of a woman, born under the Law . . . so that we might receive adoption as sons. And because you are sons, God has sent the Spirit of His Son into our hearts, crying, 'Abba! Father!' So through God you are no longer a slave but a son, and if a son, then an heir."

What amazing love! "See what love the Father has given us, that we should be called the children of God; and so we are" (1 John 3:1). (Here I prefer the old translation: "Behold what manner of love.")

Ask yourself, "When did my parents start loving me?" Ask your teen-agers. I have. It doesn't take them long before they say, "I suppose it was before I was born." Ask young parents and they will quickly affirm that they loved the baby long before it was born.

It is even more so with God. "For Thou didst form my inward parts, Thou didst knit me together in my mother's womb. I praise Thee, for Thou art fearful and wonderful. Wonderful are Thy works! Thou knowest me right well; my frame was not hidden from Thee when I was made in secret." (Ps. 139:13-15)

"In this is love, not that we loved God but that He loved us and sent His Son to be the expiation for our sins." (1 John 4:10)

Like the Father He is, He loved us long ago, and

He never quits. "I have loved you with an everlasting love. Therefore I have continued my faithfulness to you." (Jer. 31:3)

Just as a child learns to love by being loved, so we learn love this same way. "We love because He first loved us." (1 John 4:19)

"You yourselves have been taught by God to love one another." (1 Thess. 4:9)

When I have such a Father and have a home in His family, then I have no problem with "identity." I don't need to run around frantically looking for meaning for my life.

I know who I am!

Chapter THREE

BORN, then what?

We are born alone, but we grow with others.

Although there is nothing a baby can do to get born, *there is much he can do to stay born,* with the help of the parents and others in the family. Here is where my effort and my response have a part to play, though even then dependent on the Father. "For God is at work in you both to will and to work for His good pleasure." (Phil. 2:13)

Once there is life there must be growth or the new life shrivels. The primary need of the newborn is for food, and so a baby hollers until fed. Should we not feel the same hunger to be fed in our Father's household? "Like newborn babes, long for the pure spiritual milk, that you may grow up to salvation; for you have tasted the kindness of the Lord" (1 Peter 2:2-3). If our life in the family of the forgiven is to develop normally and grow strong, useful to the Father and gratifying to ourselves, we must be regularly nourished and cared for in the family circle. "You search the Scriptures, because you think that in them you have eternal life; and it is they that bear witness of Me" (John 5:39). "Jesus said to them, 'I am the Bread of Life; he who comes to Me shall not hunger, and he who believes in Me shall never thirst. . . . I am the Living Bread which came down from heaven; if anyone eats this Bread, he will live forever; and the bread which I shall give for the life of the world is My flesh.'" (John 6:35, 51)

Is the reason that so many of us grow up both anemic and uncertain in our faith due to the fact that we early develop a sporadic appetite and feed irregularly? What is the tempo of your hunger for the Word of God? Does it assert itself so as to drive you to eat regularly, or do you eat occasionally only because you know you ought to? The former is a mark of health. The latter indicates sickness.

Could it also be that we do not see enough of the love of God demonstrated in the family circle, where we should most certainly find it? Love grows out of the experience of being loved. The assurance that we have of the Father's love must also be made more firm by the actions and the care for us, by the experience we have with other members of the family.

Do we go for long periods of time without reading or hearing the Word or sharing the Lord in Communion? A vital part of anyone's growth within a family is mealtime, when all are gathered at the father's table. If one of the children doesn't show up when the meal is announced, he is called again, or one of the others is sent after him. Eating together has been a prime factor in cementing relationships in almost every civilization through the centuries of human history, and it remains a fundamental part of growing up in your own home. It is a time of joy.

Our Lord, through whom we know the Father, has given us a special invitation, urging us to be regular at His Table, where He shares Himself with us and deepens our bonds with Him so we can rejoice and be strong. We cannot miss it without weakening, but how often we do!

When you miss a meal, it is usually because you are sick or angry or away from home. It is a clear indication that something is wrong. So also in God's house. There is no better barometer of the weather in your life than your Communion attendance. When the pressure is low, the storms are coming.

What kind of family would yours be if over half of the children hardly ever came to the table? If one snacked a little at the kitchen counter and then quickly ran off to his own affairs, another took his plate to sit day after day in front of the television set, and another repeatedly said, "I'm not hungry"? And if no one ever says, "Thank you for the dinner," the house is full of ingrates.

"Ho, everyone who thirsts, come to the waters; and he who has no money, come, buy and eat! Come, buy wine and milk without money and without price. Why do you spend your money for that which is not bread, and your labor for that which does not satisfy? Hearken diligently to Me, and eat what is good, and delight yourselves in fatness. Incline your ear, and come to Me; hear, that your soul may live." (Is. 55:1-3)

Regular eating is important to growth. But so is activity, putting the nourishment to use, what the apostle Paul calls "walking in the light."

A happy child is one who has learned the discipline of obedience while wrapped in the certainty that he is loved. This does not happen suddenly or all at once. It comes from being daily under the watchful eye and loving care of the Father. "Morning by morning He wakens, He wakens my ear to hear as those who are taught. The Lord has opened my ear, and I was not rebellious. I turned not backward" (Is. 50:4-5). "Be imitators of God, as beloved children. And walk in love, as Christ loved us and gave Himself up for us" (Eph. 5:1-2). We have all seen how little ones imitate their parents when they are growing in the contentment of being loved. This is how they learn the language of the household and become the "little helpers" we so often call them. We bathe our tiny tots daily, not only to protect their health but also to develop habits and attitudes. The greeting in the morning and the kiss at night are all a part of learning the language of the family and of "growing in grace."

A verse in the Book of Proverbs (23:26) has meant a great deal to me through the years. In it the Father spoke to me, as I am sure He has spoken to many of us. "My son, give Me your heart, and let your eyes observe My ways." It is this process of getting to know the Father as He captures my heart, becoming acquainted with His ways and trying them myself as I live and move among His children in the household of faith, that can gradually imprint on us His image and make us more like Him. It is called by the big word "sanctification," which means being shaped to His design.

Trust and obedience are closely linked together in life and in the Scriptures. In fact the Bible uses the two words interchangeably in several places. Particularly in John 3:36, where Jesus says: "He who believes the Son has eternal life, but he who does not obey the Son shall not see life, but the wrath of God rests upon him." And in John 14:15: "If you love Me, you will keep My commandments." Again: "Whoever does the will of My Father in heaven is My brother and sister and mother" (Matt. 12:50; Mark 3:35). Paul advises: "Obey your parents in the Lord, for this is right"

(Eph. 6:1). We have paid too little attention to the close relationship between trust and obedience, and as a consequence it is not easy for others to see our Lord's likeness in us.

Ask a youth group, when you have their minds going, "Are there rules in your house? Why? How do you look at the rules? What if there were no rules? Would you like it that way? Would you be happier then? Are rules tyranny, or love?"

They will usually answer that if their folks made no rules whatever, they would be unsure of their love. It would be a sign that they did not care at all about them. We are not talking about a lot of little petty laws that are an unexplained irritation in some households, but the basic rules for living in our homes and in the family of the forgiven. He who designed our life also has the responsibility to announce the fundamental rules for its healthful and happy operation, just as the manufacturer of a car must issue a manual for its successful use. If you buy a car and then throw away the operating manual, saying, "Who needs oil? I'll use vinegar. It's *my* car and I can do with it as I please," you are in for trouble. We of course are not a manufactured article, but the principle still holds. We must learn to live within the family.

What is the significance of the verse in Prov. 13:24: "He who spares the rod hates his son, but he who loves him is diligent to discipline him"?

And look at Heb. 12:8: "If you are left without discipline, in which all have participated, then you are illegitimate children and not sons." The family where each does only as he pleases and thinks only of himself soon disintegrates.

How important is it to understand the reasons behind a parent's words? Obviously they are important to any partnership in the house. Does understanding increase in value as we grow? Isn't it through constant conversation that we grow in understanding, both in our own homes and with the Father in his family? Talk these things over in your family circle.

Are there times when one simply has to trust the command, even though one does not understand the reason? Have you listened to a youngster calling in the back yard to a brother or sister?

"You have to come in now."

"Why?"

"Because Daddy says!"

For a happy child, who knows he is loved and who is learning to put trust and obedience together, this is usually enough. Sometimes it is all we have to go on.

What is the punch in the episode involving Peter in Luke 5:4-10? You remember that Peter was a fisherman by trade. He had fished this lake all his life and knew all the holes, the weed beds, and every shelf along the shore. He was a good judge of the best time to fish. They had fished all night, which evidently was the best time for that lake, and now in broad daylight Jesus tells them to let down their nets.

Peter says, "We have fished all night and caught nothing." In other words, "It won't work."

How often have you and I said the same thing when Christ through His Word or His Spirit suggested something which we did not think would work, or which we were disinclined to do? We would rather go by our own judgments, or we bring all sorts of excuses.

If Peter had only said, "I don't think it will work," and nothing more, I wonder what sort of life his would have been? But he said one thing more, and this made a tremendous difference.

He said, "Nevertheless, at your word I will do it." And look what happened!

"Because You say so!"

I wonder how much joy we miss, how many good spiritual hunches are killed by logical argument. I wonder how many deep spiritual experiences we lose out on because we so seldom are willing to say, "Because You say so I will do it." The fruits of simple obedience are spoiled by the wormy core of selfish reasoning.

When I know His love, I can live in the kind of trust that says, "Because You say so," but it takes a lot of growing in grace.

Chapter FOUR

my Father's name— and mine

As soon as he is born, a child *is* a son in the family, but in a sense he must also *become* a son in the household.

As we live within the embrace of a family and experience the care we get from our parents in the little things of every day, we grow into a consciousness of who we are and to whom we belong. Looking back, it is difficult to say just when or how we came into a personal realization of this identity, or belonging, but it is a very real part of personal development.

I remember so well a Sunday school Christmas program back in the days when they were still popular, when a girl of 4 or 5 climbed the chancel steps to say her piece, having been steered in that direction by her teacher. She looked the audience over searchingly, then she broke into a smile, raised her hand, and pointed: "There's my pop!"

This was the important thing. Then she spoke her piece and trotted down contented.

What a privilege to grow in the knowledge that He who wakens me morning by morning is my Father, who "keeps me as the apple of His eye"! "His eye is on the sparrow, and I know He watches me."

In Rom. 8:15 we are told that it is the work of the Holy Spirit to bring into our hearts the consciousness of sonship, so that we will naturally say "Abba! Father!"—"There's my pop!" Is this why Jesus said, "Unless you become like children, you cannot become a part of the kingdom"?

There are those who take it so for granted that they miss the joy of gratitude, and gradually the sense of really being His own fades and diminishes. Others are so uncertain that if asked, "Are you a child of God?" they answer, "I hope so, I have tried to do what is right." For them the Christian life has become mostly a list of things forbidden. They are like the little boy who was asked his name and replied:

"Johnny."

"Johnny what?"

"Johnny Don't."

There cannot be much exuberance in this kind of relationship, and it certainly is not the way our Father wants it to be with us. How much better the delightful excitement of "There's my pop!"

I carry my Father's name.

My human surname is important to my whole existence. It identifies me and to whom I belong. When I was a young one running around the community, people recognized me as "Ingvald Daehlin's boy." Who my father was also rubbed off on me. People were inclined to think of me in the light of my father's name. His place in the community affected mine, and I could draw on his reputation.

As time went by, what I did and how I behaved also had some effect on how my father's name was thought of in the town. If I get to thinking that I can act as I momentarily please, without its affecting others—my father and his friends and the rest of the family—I have become both blind and selfish, and I dishonor my father's name. *With identity comes responsibility.*

It is significant that the commandment "Honor thy father and thy mother" is the only one to which there is a specific promise attached: "That it may be well with thee and thou mayest live long upon the earth." We cannot separate this "honoring" from our whole person, our total attitude, and make it something we *perform* on occasion, apart from an intimate, everyday relationship.

God says in Is. 43:1: "Fear not, I have redeemed you; I have called you by name, you are Mine." I carry my Father's name when I am a child of God. I am a child of the King, and His name brings with it the assurance of who I am, where I belong, under whom I live, and where I am heading.

I need not be lost or without purpose!

We carry the name "children of God" and the name "Christian," which originated in the same way—those who belong to Christ. Jesus Christ is the Head of the church, the community of the redeemed, the family of the forgiven. Their life with Him gave them the name Christian. With his sign—the cross—we are sealed as His own in Baptism. Our lives witness to this name. Perhaps that is what Paul had in mind when he wrote in Col. 3:15-17: "And let the peace of Christ rule in your hearts, to which indeed you were called in one body. And be thankful. Let the Word of Christ dwell in you richly as you teach and admonish one another in all wisdom . . . . And whatever you do, in word or deed, do everything in the name of the Lord Jesus, giving thanks to God the Father through Him."

If my life in my Father's house is to have any genuine joy and meaning, He must talk with me and I with Him.

We bemoan the fact that there is a great communications gap between parents and children in our generation, and that they cannot, or at least do not, talk with each other or listen to each other.

From this situation spring many of the ills of our society.

What is it like in the household of faith—the church? Do many of our ills and weaknesses also come from the same situation—a communications gap?

Our Father speaks to us and wants us to hear what He has to say because His Word has eternal significance for our lives, both now and forever. If the words of Christ "dwell in us richly," they will shape our character, influence our thinking, and affect our decisions. We know from the effect of TV commercials that words engraved on the mind through repetition definitely come into play when decisions are made. The more of the Word of God we store in our memories, the more it will affect what we are and do and say. But it is easy to be deafened by the noise and chaff of this world. I had an uncle, Mike, who had become quite deaf. When the doctor removed nearly an inch-long column of packed dust from his ear canal, he heard again. It had packed in there through years of sitting on the corn binder.

Our Father is also eager to hear what we have to say to Him. Surely He "knows what we need before we ask" (Matt. 6:8). When we falter and do not find words to express what is on our hearts, "the Spirit helps us in our weakness; for we do not know how to pray as we ought, but the Spirit

Himself intercedes for us with sighs too deep for words" (Rom. 8:26). This is certainly true, for there are many times when we do not know what to say to the Father, or just how to say it. There are times when all you can say is, "Father, help me!" At such times we may not be sure of much more than that "underneath are the everlasting arms." It is good, then, to know that we have the Holy Spirit pleading our case.

There is real strength in the habit of talking with the Father, anytime, anywhere, freely and naturally. What kind of relationship would a son have with his father if he talked to him only when he was in deep trouble and scared, or when there was some handout he wanted for himself? It wouldn't be very satisfying on either side.

Isn't this the way our conversation with our heavenly Father tends to be? It is amazing how hard it is to maintain regular family devotions. It must be because Satan knows that this is where real bonds develop between our Father and His children and between various members of the family. Therefore if he can maintain a communications gap in this area, he has half the battle won. And why is the habit of talking naturally to the Father so difficult to pass on to our own children so it will become a treasured part of their daily lives when they marry? Is it because for too many decades the language of prayer has been an archaic holdover from the Middle Ages and is not the way we converse today? Is it because we are embarrassed to ask our guests to join us in prayer when we have them in for dinner? One can make a long list of things that interfere, even in a pastor's house. In our home you could bet the phone would ring sometime during our devotions at the supper table. Is there a more effective way than family devotions to help the youngsters who are growing up in our family circle get the habit of thinking about each other, and the whole wide world, as they talk to God?

There is no unwillingness to hear on the part of our Father. He has repeatedly said, "Come to Me," "Let us reason together," which is another way of saying, "Let's have a chat."

I think one of the finest pieces of writing outside of the Bible is the little explanation of the introduction to the Lord's Prayer in Luther's Small Catechism:

"Our Father who art in heaven."

"What does this mean?"

"God thereby tenderly encourages us to believe that He is truly our Father and we are truly His children, and that we can come to Him boldly and confidently in prayer as beloved children come to their dear father."

Let me put it in more everyday words: "God invites and urges us to come and talk to Him freely and confidently like any well-loved youngster comes to talk with a loving dad."

This has helped me when I have felt hampered or tongue-tied in prayer. It also settles the question of what you can or should pray about. He says to come just as you are with all that is on your heart and mind, without any hesitancy or reservation, just as you want your own kids to freely come to you. No particular time is designated or any formal approach needed. We come in Jesus' name because He has opened the door. He has made the whole thing possible. "No one comes to the Father but by Me" (John 14:6). Look up. He's there, like your father walking next to you, only better, for He can even hear your yearning. Life is solid then. Even when it gets banged around it's solid.

"For this reason I bow my knees before the Father, from whom every family in heaven and on earth is named, that according to the riches of His glory He may grant you to be strengthened through His Spirit in the inner man, and that Christ may dwell in your hearts through faith; that you, being rooted and grounded in love, may have power to comprehend with all the saints what is the breadth and length and height and depth and to know the love of Christ, which surpasses knowledge, that you may be filled with all the fullness of God." (Eph. 3:14-19)

He has given us His name. We belong to Him,

and in this belonging lies our peace. It is together with all the others in the family that we learn to comprehend the full measure of His love, to know some of its dimensions as we share it with others.

PAX

Chapter FIVE

Forgiven and Forgiving

The practice of mercy is the heart of a happy home. It is also the mark of the family of the forgiven.

We became members of our human families through the gift of life from our parents. This life developed into a conscious relationship of love as we grew in the home. The happiness of the home rests on the continuity of this relationship. When the child's behavior strains or damages this relationship, it must be restored through forgiveness, or there is no peace. Without this restoration the members of the family become gradually estranged from each other.

But it is not easy to say, "I'm sorry."

We became part of God's family through the regenerative power of His forgiveness in Christ. We grow in that family by living in this state of forgiveness, daily renewed. We respond to His mercy by learning in the family to be merciful to each other and to all men. This is our calling and our life.

First we must live with our Father as forgiven children. This is not just a one-time event, but a continually renewed relationship. We fall so far short of what He meant us to be, and our nature is such that we stand in need of being constantly cleansed by His pardon. Where there is offense, there is also estrangement until the offense is cleared away in pardon. His heart yearns for my return and restoration. It is the work of the Holy Spirit in our hearts to bring us to the decision to go to Him in confession for the healing of the rift. He pleads with His children: "Return, O Israel, to the Lord your God, for you have stumbled because of your iniquity. *Take with you words* and return unto the Lord; say to Him: 'Take away all iniquity.'" (Hos. 14:1-2)

Jesus brought this out in the story of the prodigal son, where, though the father longed for the son's return, the moment of truth was when the young man came to his senses and said to himself, "I'm going back to my father." The psalmist sings it beautifully in Ps. 32:5: "I said, 'I will confess my transgressions to the Lord'; then Thou didst forgive the guilt of my sin."

The crucial factor, "taking with you words" and going to the Father, is our primary need.

In any loving family it should be a natural

thing for a child to come confidently to his parent to be renewed in pardon. Then why do we so often hesitate?

It should also be the most natural thing in the life of any believer to come expectantly to God for forgiveness. Jesus has assured us that He will not break a bent reed nor snuff out a flickering wick. "Him who comes to Me I will not cast out" (John 6:37). "If we confess our sins, He is faithful and just and will forgive our sins and cleanse us from all unrighteousness" (1 John 1:9). What could be more assuring than promises like these? And yet it seems so hard to do. The sense of guilt is there. The yearning for repair lies underneath, but how difficult it is to go about getting the rift mended!

We all know from our own houses how disruptive of peace and joy in the home it is if one youngster keeps picking at another. It is not enough that the children are in good graces with their folks. They must also practice mercy with each other.

I asked a group of young people once (and they were the cream of the crop—40 selected youth from more than two states):

"Are there any rifts that occur in your families?"

"Oh, yes!" And they proceeded to describe the hurts, the offenses, and the thoughtlessness that so easily happen in our home life.

Then I asked: "What do you do about them? How do you go about mending the rifts in your house?"

A profound silence! No one said a word.

This was puzzling because there had been no reticence in the discussion so far. Obviously this was something new. About the best they could come up with was that one tries to be extra nice for a while, hoping that the strain would disappear and the hurt somehow would no longer be there.

Does this mean that in our homes and families we seldom "take with us words" and return to a brother seeking pardon and healing in our everyday life? Do we merely silently hope that everything will eventually right itself? Is the best we can think of the phrase "I goofed"?

How about, "I'm sorry. Forgive me," and the loving answer, "Of course." That is the key to life.

One who is truly forgiven, who has absorbed God's mercy, must also become forgiving. The whole thrust of the picture drawn by Jesus in Matthew 18 points this out. The man who had just been freed from an impossible debt "because he asked" went out and throttled a fellow servant who owed him a small debt. He did not let the pardon change him. This action revealed a heart that did not appropriate the healing power of the pardon just granted him. He would not show the same mercy to his brother, so he lost his own. It had never taken hold in him. "So also My heavenly Father will do to every one of you, if you do not forgive your brother from your heart." (Matt. 18:35)

We cannot separate God's mercy from ours. When we receive mercy, the result must be that we in turn become merciful. "Be merciful, even as your Father is merciful. Judge not, and you will not be judged; condemn not, and you will not be condemned; forgive, and you will be forgiven." (Luke 6:36-37)

The practice of mercy with each other is so related to our peace with our Father that Jesus illustrated it this way: "If you are offering your gift at the altar and there remember that your brother has something against you, leave your gift before the altar and go; first be reconciled to your brother, and then come and offer your gift." (Matt. 5:23-24)

The familiar phrase in the Lord's Prayer, which we "repeat" thoughtlessly so often, brings out the same point, that being forgiven and becoming forgiving are very closely related.

This interpersonal relationship, founded on the same kind of mercy that the Father gives us, is so fundamental to our life in the family of the forgiven that it is repeatedly emphasized in the New Testament.

In Matt. 7:4 and Luke 6:42 Jesus puts His finger on our habit of picking at the little sliver faults of others while we have a logjam in our own eyes. He warns against being angry with a brother and throwing nasty words at him (Matt. 5:22-24). He desires that the way in which He looks at us and deals with us become mirrored in our feeling toward His other children, our brothers. When we forgive, we have truly experienced the healing power of being forgiven.

The Jews had it all worked out according to scale. By their system you could perform a function without investing your heart. It was all written down in rules. You were supposed to forgive a person three times, that was all that was required. Peter, having been with Jesus, sensed that this was the wrong dimension. The measure was not nearly enough. So he wanted to know what the limit was to the practice of mercy.

"Lord, how many times shall my brother sin against me and I forgive him? Is seven times enough?"

Jesus answered that there was to be no limit. Our Father has set the scope of forgiveness in His total mercy to us, and Paul says in Col. 3:13: "As the Lord has forgiven you, so you also must forgive." It is not a matter of how many times, but how you feel toward your brother.

One can go through the motions and even say the words and yet spoil the whole thing by not doing it, as Jesus says, from the heart. When I was a youngster in boarding school, fifth grade, another boy and I were required to beg a teacher's pardon for some classroom shenanigans. We were not very sorry at the time. A schoolmate put it into our heads to say:

"Beg your pardon, grant your grace.

Hope the cat will lick your face."

We found out that this kind of repentance doesn't work. The heart must be involved.

Being imitators of God in the practice of mercy does not come easily. We gladly accept the abundant mercy with which the Father treats us, but to beg a pardon and to freely grant it to one another in the daily give-and-take of life in the household of faith is not so quickly learned. It takes a great deal of the transforming work of the Holy Spirit.

Surely, the heavenly Father need never seek His children's pardon, for He is perfect goodness. But in the human family the need to seek pardon is sometimes a two-way street. Parents have faults, too, and may need at times to seek a child's forgiveness so that both sides of the rift can be brought together. This is one difference in the Biblical analogy which the human father needs to remember. If we are willing to risk our stance, great things can happen in the home.

We put on a little skit one night at family camp in the Rockies. Young and old were there, and we were on the subject of mending hurts. Prior to the meeting we had searched the kitchen for a dish towel that had seen its best days and tore easily. The dish towel was hung in front of the lectern. A friend came up and took hold of one corner, I grasped the other corner, and we started off in different directions. It tore half way down. We turned our backs to each other, offended. Then we both thought it over. Each of us picked up a large needle threaded with heavy red thread. My friend stitched up only his side of the tear. Then I stitched up only my side. When we had done this, I turned to the audience and said, "We fixed it, didn't we?"

The children in the group responded in a chorus, "No you didn't. You have to sew both sides together again."

We know better than we do.

The practice of mercy is the mark of the family of the forgiven. It is exactly on this level that the world around us judges us too, and it is here that our witness to the love of God becomes the strongest, or the weakest.

Neighbors watch our families. The world watches the church to see if the love of God finds expression in the practice of mercy.

There was a kettle merchant named Wang in a Chinese village who had a terrible temper. His wife started attending classes at the mission chapel down the street simply to avoid his tirades and to get an hour or two of peace. She became a believer, and the result in her life so impressed her husband that he had her teach him everything she had learned each day when she came home. By this method he memorized the entire Catechism and grew into a living faith.

Shortly after he had been baptized, someone stole one of his kettles. Ordinarily this would have sent Mr. Wang down the village street loudly cursing whoever stole his kettle. Added to this would be a shouted threat that if the kettle were not returned within an hour, he would come back and curse the culprit's ancestors too. Putting the curse on ancestors was considered the ultimate insult.

Instead of cursing the length of the street, Mr. Wang went to the chapel and asked the evangelist to pray with him so that he would not resort to cursing. A couple of days later a neighbor brought back his kettle, saying: "You really are a Christian, aren't you?"

It is in forgiving that the family of the forgiven becomes a healing community. The practice of mercy has transforming power. God help us to use it more!

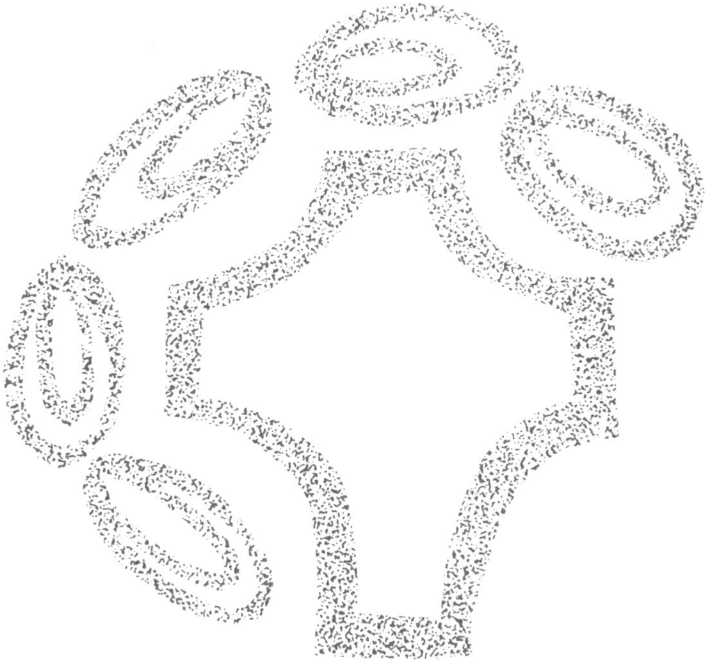

Chapter SIX

care for the others

The function of a family is to respond to the parents' love by caring for each other. The baby is fed and tended by someone else. The toddler who crosses the street is held by a stronger hand. The one who is learning something new is assisted by one with more experience, and the one who is hurt is comforted by the rest. Those who have an accomplishment to report are rejoiced with. When someone is sick he is tended, for no one is completely well until the sick one is back on his feet again. Those who are away for a while are missed and longed for and written to. Little hurts are kissed away. And this *is* part of the balm of Gilead.

"Two are better than one, because they have a good reward for their toil. For if they fall, one will lift up his fellow; but woe to him who is alone when he falls and has not another to lift him up." (Eccl. 4:9)

A social worker in one of our big cities asked the mother of a large family of children which one she loved the most. After a moment she replied, "The one who is sick, until he is well, and the one who is away, until he is home." It could not have been put better. I read this long ago, and it has been with me ever since.

So also with the household of faith. This is the kind of love the Father has for *you*. Our Lord said: "This is My commandment, that you love one another as I have loved you" (John 15:12). "Let love be genuine; hate what is evil, hold fast to what is good; love one another with brotherly affection; outdo one another in showing honor. . . . Rejoice with those who rejoice, weep with those who weep." (Rom. 12:9-10, 15)

It is impossible to separate love of the Father from love of the brother. "If anyone says, 'I love God,' and hates his brother, he is a liar; for he who does not love his brother whom he has seen, cannot love God whom he has not seen." (1 John 4:20-21)

Knit together by love from the Father and love for each other, we become one body and are "members of one another," so that "if one member suffers, all suffer together; if one member is honored, all rejoice together." It is God's design that "the members may have the same care for one another." (1 Cor. 12:26 and 25)

What about the members of the household of faith who are missing? There are many of them, and the rest of us do very little about it.

Can you imagine a family, yours or mine, that goes on a picnic in the woods. After lunch everyone is having fun, and the afternoon passes quickly. Soon it is time to go home. The gear is packed in the trunk of the car. Dad whistles for the kids, and everyone piles in. Just before the key is turned to start the motor, heads are counted, and it turns out that Jimmy's missing. Can you imagine such a family saying:

"Well, that's his hard luck. I'm hungry and tired. Let's go home."

Never!

Instead, the entire tribe would be mobilized in a search that would end only when Jimmy had been found and was back again where he belonged.

"Like a bird that strays from its nest is a man who strays from his home." (Prov. 27:8)

Some of us remember the nationwide attention when a small boy in western North Dakota strayed from his home some years ago. (And there are frequent incidents like this reported in the papers.) The entire community got together for the search. People joined in from neighboring towns. They linked hands, forming long lines, and combed the prairies and the brush, every hill and every coulee, so that they would not miss a foot of ground until the boy was found and brought back to his home.

What would it be like if we had this kind of concern in the church? It would be a new day, wouldn't it? And there would be rejoicing in heaven.

"It is not the will of My Father who is in heaven that one of these little ones should perish." (Matt. 18:14)

"What man of you, having a hundred sheep, if he has lost one of them, does not leave the ninety-nine in the wilderness and go after the one which is lost, until he finds it? And when he has found it, he lays it on his shoulders, rejoicing. And when he comes home, he calls together his friends and neighbors, saying to them, 'Rejoice with me, for I have found my sheep which was lost." (Luke 15:3-6)

But look at us in the family of the forgiven! More than half are missing when the family gets together to worship the Father on Sunday. Many have been gone for a long time. Do we care enough to find them?

There isn't one of us who cannot think of someone who was not there the last time we gathered at the Father's table. Did it burden our hearts so that we did something about it? Or did we climb into the family car, saying, "Well, that's their hard luck. I'm tired and hungry. Let's go home — there's a football game on television."

Some have not come to our fellowship or study group lately. Did we find out why? Did we search for them? Call them up? Many of the youth haven't been around for some time. Have I gone to them or tried to discover why they stopped coming? Do the other young people look them up and bring them back? If they were asked, would they say, "No one seems to care whether I'm home anyway?"

" 'I was hungry and you gave Me no food, I was thirsty and you gave Me no drink, I was a stranger and you did not welcome Me, naked and you did not clothe Me, sick and in prison and you did not visit Me.' Then they also will answer, 'Lord, when did we see Thee hungry or thirsty or a stranger or naked or sick or in prison and did not minister to Thee?' Then He will answer them, 'Truly, I say to you, as you did it not to one of the least of these, you did it not to Me.' " (Matt. 25:24-25)

One of the earliest questions asked of man was the one God directed to Cain, "Where is Abel your brother?" The question is still being asked and is as modern as today. We ask it of our children often. Our Father keeps asking it of us. We *are* each other's keepers in a family.

When we *do* care, when we *do* develop a compassionate companionship, our own sense of belonging is buttressed, our love can grow, our joys are deepened, others become more sure of their identity and their worth, the Father's name is honored, and the family is strengthened.

Look at what happened to Thomas right after Easter. The event is recorded in John 20:24-29. It is hard to imagine how crushed Thomas was when he saw Jesus die. All his hopes for the restoration of Israel had now suddenly been wiped out. The Master, to whom he had committed himself and on whom he had pinned his hopes, was dead. This kind of loss was impossible to understand and hard to accept.

In his despair Thomas evidently went off by himself somewhere, so that he was not with the rest of the disciples when the risen Lord appeared to them, and *he nearly missed life!*

How often we do the same! When in a bind, depressed or defeated, hurt or confused, we stray off from the community of believers, nursing our problem in dismal silence. Confining ourselves to our own little life orbit, we get to feeling that no one cares, and we even begin to blame God. When we cut ourselves off from the support and help that the family of believers can give, we isolate our loneliness and block the help we so desperately need and want. There are lots of faults in that company of faith, for sure, but they have a strength too, given by the Father who is in their midst, and it can be found by the wounded seeker.

One wonders what would have become of Thomas if he had remained in this condition? If he had stayed away, holed up by himself. But he did one thing that changed his life. The next week he was back in the congregation, and he became a new person.

What brought him back?

The Scriptures do not tell us, but we can imagine a bit. Did one of the other disciples bring him along that next week? I like to believe that there was someone, maybe several, who cared enough when they saw that Thomas was not there the night that Jesus came, and who then asked around until they found him. When they had looked him up they told him about seeing the risen Christ.

Thomas was a typical modern-day practical man. He voiced his doubts and laid down a lot of conditions, but nevertheless he was back again with the community of believers the next week, and there he saw the Lord—and believed.

Notice as you read the passage how gently Jesus deals with him. He picks him up right where he is. There is no chiding or scolding. Thomas is accepted the way he is, with all his doubts and his stubborness, and met at the point of his need.

I can come to my Lord, too, with all my inner turmoil, my fears, questions, disappointments and doubts, and all my longings. He is able to heal. He is available; but best of all, He is utterly approachable. He will meet me right where I am and touch also me at the point of my need.

When Thomas saw this and beheld the living Lord, he said, "My Lord and my God!" Tradition tells us that Thomas later became a pioneer missionary to India. Others in the family had cared about him, and this made the difference between defeat and victory. You never know how far the results will reach when you stretch out a loving hand.

But there is more.

As we grow in Christ, our Father will expand our vision and extend our hearts to see that he intends *all men* to be in his family. This, too, is the Father's business.

"He desires all men to be saved and come to the knowledge of the truth." (1 Tim. 2:4)

Once we begin to "comprehend with all the saints what is the breadth and length and height and depth of His love" and realize that there is absolutely no one left out, that Jesus died for all that all might live in Him, then reaching out with His redeeming love to all men begins to possess our minds and impel our hearts. His aim can become ours, that there be "one flock, one Shepherd," one family of the forgiven, growing in Christ.

"And I have other sheep that are not of this fold; I must bring them also, and they will heed My voice. So there shall be one flock, one Shepherd." (John 10:16)

"My brethren, if anyone among you wanders from the truth and someone brings him back, let him know that whoever brings back a sinner from the error of his way will save his soul from death and will cover a multitude of sins." (James 5:19-20)

Andrew brought his brother Peter to Jesus. Philip went and found his friend Nathanael. Down through the centuries this is how the Master has reclaimed multitudes, one by one. What should be more natural than bringing home a brother or a friend? And yet how afraid we are to try!

Maybe we have had it too easy. Like many modern-day families in affluent times, there is so much machinery to depend on that we think the machinery or the program will do it, so we leave it up to someone else. Like true Americans, we elect a committee for everything.

Not until some tragedy strikes, or some great loss is suffered, or some trial faced, do we discover again the sustaining power of the household of faith. Maybe the Father will have to allow us to enter into some suffering before we begin to hold each other's hand and reach out to others who sit with a handful of their own longings and wait for a knock on the door.

"May those who sow in tears reap with shouts of joy! He that goes forth weeping, bearing the seed for sowing, shall come home with shouts of joy, bringing his sheaves with him." (Ps. 126:5-6)

Jesus said that He had come that we might have life *abundantly* and that His joy might be ours. The walls of His household should reverberate with laughter, for the heart of the forgiven can shout for joy, and for every wanderer who is brought back to his home there must be rejoicing both in heaven and on earth.

But remember, "Apart from Me you can do nothing." (John 15:5)

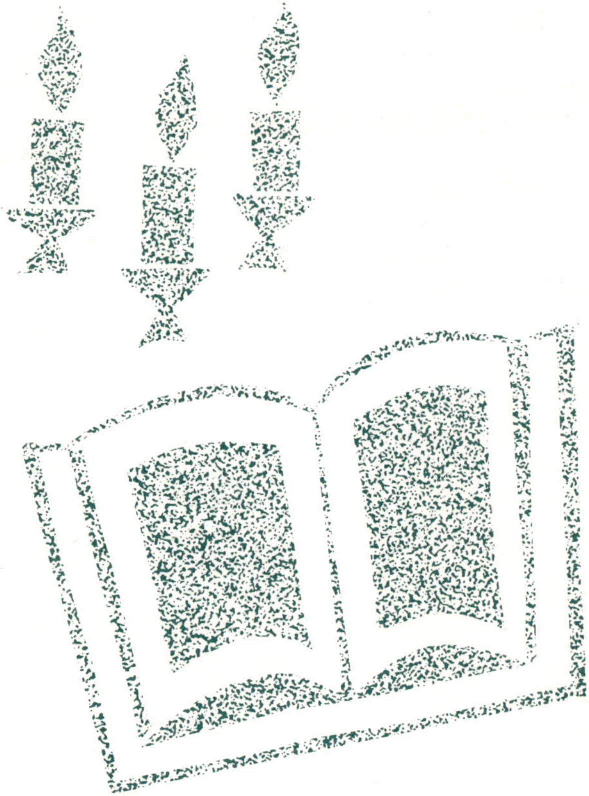

Chapter SEVEN

Surrogate Father
(the priest in your house)

A surrogate is a person appointed to act in the place of another. As "surrogate fathers" we are therefore God's appointed representatives in the lives of our young children.

A father teaches his child to throw a ball, ride a bike, drop a line, row a boat, run a motor, drive a car, and many other things. In the course of the years he also transmits to his children his own sense of values. It is not only what he says but what he does and what he is that affects the life and thought of his children.

We who are fathers play a vital role in giving to our young their earliest ideas of God. Educators and psychologists tell us that a child's early experiences with his earthly father profoundly affect his inner concept of the heavenly Father. This should give us fathers some sober thoughts, and also inspire some thorough dedication. It is an awesome position to be in. The trouble is that we can't duck out of it. One way or another we will be partners in the shaping of our child's concept of God the Father.

Which way will we tip the scales?

First of all, through his own father a child can early know what it is to be loved and cared for, to understand the peace of belonging. Conversely, he may learn indifference, resentment, alienation. and even hate.

One of the things we used to try in our confirmation classes in a congregation where I served was to get an idea of the sort of picture our confirmands had of their own fathers' relationship to the family. We would put a word on the board, asking them to say immediately what came to mind as the word was written.

The word was "father."

The class would volunteer all sorts of things: "He is strong. He protects you. He cares for you. He takes you fishing. He makes money and buys things. He makes you mind."

One year when I wrote the word "father" on the board, one of the boys whispered between his teeth: "Hate." How could a lad who felt this way begin to pray, "Our Father who art in heaven"?

With some special care from the pastor, after class, he began to describe the kind of father he would like to have, and his face lit up. From then on he was able to get something out of his confirmation studies.

This was certainly an extreme case, but what about the thousands of young people today who say, "My folks never talk about these things," or, "I can't talk to my parents. They are too busy to care what I think. We never talk about spiritual things at home."

Paul admonishes in Eph. 6:4: "Fathers, do not provoke your children to wrath, but bring them up in the discipline and instruction of the Lord."

On the positive side, what a privilege it is to be the one to introduce your son to the heavenly Father and help him live securely in the knowledge that he is loved by God! Our most lasting joys will come from having succeeded in this introduction.

"I write to you, fathers, because you know Him who is from the beginning. I write to you, young men, because you are strong, and the Word of God abides in you, and you have overcome the evil one" (1 John 2:14). The apostle John, in his letter of love, addresses the fathers and the young men in this way, and he repeats the address.

When you know the Lord, you are strong, and your family looks to you for this strength. It is from you that they learn things that are considered important. You are the one who brings them into a sense of security through steady love and discipline and by what you are.

Dads, especially the young men who are starting families, you are the priests in your houses by divine appointment.

"Be yourselves built into a spiritual house, to be a holy priesthood." (1 Peter 2:5)

"Only take heed and keep your soul diligently, lest you forget the things which your eyes have seen, and lest they depart from your heart all the days of your life; make them known to your children and your children's children." (Deut. 4:9)

The priest's function was to teach, lead in worship, and plead for his people.

When God dealt with Israel, speaking to them through His servant Moses, and made them a covenant people, it was to the heads of the families that He spoke.

The father's place as priest and teacher in his own house was built into the celebration of the Passover, the most important event of the year. At this feast, which commemorated Israel's redemption from slavery in Egypt and their return home by the power of God, a son would ask the man of the house, "Father, what is the meaning of these things?" Then the father would tell the story of the powerful acts of God that were being remembered in this feast.

By God's command it was the father who was to teach the Word to the children. "Hear, O Israel . . . these words which I command you this day shall be upon your heart; and you shall teach them diligently to your children, and shall talk of them when you sit in your house and when you walk by the way and when you lie down and when you rise" (Deut. 6:6-9). The instruction was to be woven into the everyday fabric of their lives, and the father was to play the primary role. He was both teacher and priest.

We have managed to pass the buck or deputize so many things in our American life, and as a result families have been fragmented and a solid sense of belonging to the household of faith has also eroded. Much of the certainty of belonging has been damaged when fathers leave it up to everyone else to teach their children about God and to lead them in worship. And then we wonder why they drift away?

I recall a dying man who asked me to write a letter to his grown boys. His restless anguish was that he had talked to them about many things when they were growing up, taken them fishing, and otherwise tried to be a good father, but he had not gone with them to church or talked to them about his faith in God in his own home. He had not introduced them to the Father. Now his opportunity was nearly gone, so this was his last wish.

But we need not have to later look back in regret and failure. We can have the joy of seeing our young grow up with a deep sense of belonging, knowing through us the peace of being loved and forgiven.

Of course it isn't easy. All kinds of fears assert themselves every time we think of attempting it. A variety of false images of ourselves and the cleverest evasions come to the surface. You are not alone in this. It is not unique with you. We all experience them. It is even hard in a pastor's home where we generally expect these things to be smooth and easy. Good things do not come cheap. Nevertheless, once you have broken the ice, you discover that you will not faint dead away in the process. And your entire family will remember you for it and thank God that you were that kind of dad.

You *can* "do all things through Him who strengthens you," if you ask Him for the help and then try. But you have to try!

We can learn—through study and through practice. I remember when I first started timidly caring for our first baby, feeding and changing the tiny mite. I was sure she would break in two in my knobby hands. However, a little trying made it easier until I came to feel like an old pro.

We study many things—especially in fields where we are convinced and committed. I have a book two inches thick on nothing but trout fishing, and still go back to it after many years. So also we can study our priesthood as God's surrogate fathers in our own families.

I think the easiest place to start is by helping the tiniest ones with their evening prayers, and then as they grow older sit long enough by the bed afterwards to hear what they have on their minds. That is when they tend to say many things which would not otherwise come out. It is an open door to a communion and an intimacy that will pay big dividends later, when they hit the bumps in life. Fortunate is the man who has a wife who gently pushes him into accepting this responsibility.

The father's own faithfulness at worship is a vital part of his priesthood. It is worship in church *with* his father that makes the habit last in the life of a growing boy.

There are very few children who are successfully "sent to church." If they are taken and accompanied, it might stick. You can tell them daily how important it is, but if you only *send* them, they have a right to conclude that if it is important at all it must be so only for little children. Therefore, as soon as they are older and no longer consider themselves little children, they will emulate Dad. What he does must be important. If he dodges worship and study, then worship and study cannot be important. Your children will draw these conclusions no matter what you say. It is what you *do* that will convince them. You can no more teach your boy truthfulness if you habitually lie than you could teach him electronics by reciting poetry, or teach him to fly a plane by digging in the backyard. It is the same with his church life.

And look what can happen in the framework of family devotions! Simple conversations with God led by the father in the family circle are the surest way of helping the children learn to talk naturally with their heavenly Father. Gratitude, thoughtfulness, concern for others can be brought home to them through your family prayers. My wife and I used to wonder how we could keep the "thank-you habit" in the lives of our young ones. The older they became the harder it seemed to be to remember to say thank you. As an experiment I began regularly including a thank You to God for the dinner mother had prepared. Before long the children began to say, "Thank you for the dinner, Mom," when they left the table. When a father talks to God about his children's future, that they might look forward to Christian homes and faith-filled mates, that they may know God's guidance in the choice of a profession, and the choice of friends, these things can then also become a part of their thought life and prayer life.

The young person who has had the experience of hearing himself prayed for regularly at home during his growing years will therefore live in the knowledge, after he is grown and leaves home, that his life is still sustained and undergirded by his father's continued prayers. This, more than anything else we might do or say, will work toward keeping him in the faith as the years go by. I am not guessing or dreaming. I know, because this is how it happened in my life. My own parents were on the other side of the globe when I went through my rocky and obstreperous teens, and it was the surety of their daily pleading with the Lord that held on to me.

You have been called to be the priest in your house, a surrogate father. There is no one else who can do it. Not the pastor, not your wife, not the church. Only you. For this particular responsibility almighty God is limited to only you. He has no one else.

What a day when the Lord says to you: "Well done, good and faithful servant; you have been faithful over a little, I will set you over much; enter into the joy of your Master"! (Matt. 25:21)

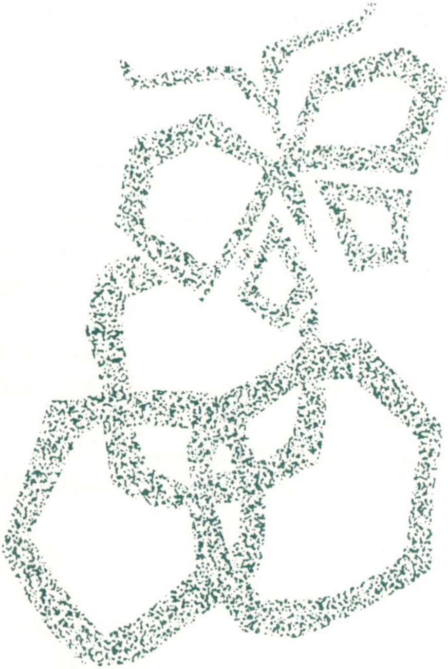

Chapter EIGHT

a tryst with the master

Why should I add this last chapter on a "tryst with the Master—the death of his saints"?

At first it doesn't seem a part of the picture of family life, but then again it surely does.

Our physical, earthly families are going to break up little by little and be transformed into something else. Some will go off to college, and the departure has begun. Some will leave to start units of their own in marriage. Some will depart this life through death—long before we can see why it should be. And eventually we will all walk through that door.

By contrast, our present unit of the family of faith looks forward to a gathering together with other units, someday, into one great family. We have an ultimate goal—to be with our Lord and to rejoice forever in the presence of our Father. Like the North Star, this goal gives us direction when the night is dark around us. There is a shifting, one by one, from a restless world to a final home, with boundaries way beyond our ken.

My family here, and yours, is the smallest unit of the greater household of faith, busy learning to be a family under the care of the Head of the house, the Lord Christ. The more fully we draw our love from Him and live it with each other, the more we become a part of one another.

God can, and does, so richly bless our life with each other under His grace that the separation through death becomes a shattering experience, leaving a present emptiness that nothing seems to be able to fill.

Where we laughed together we now cry alone.

Then the Father stoops to talk to me again. He speaks through His Word and through the hearts of others in the communion of saints, and specially through His Son, Jesus Christ, my Lord.

"You are not alone, either in tears or laughter, for I am with you. The one you loved so dearly, whose departure you see as a crushing loss, is now safe where you, too, hope one day to be."

"In My Father's house are many rooms; if it were not so, would I have told you that I go to prepare a place for you? And when I go and prepare a place for you, I will come again and will take you to Myself, that where I am you may be also." (John 14:1-3)

"Nothing can separate you from My love. Not life, not death, not anything! You can trust Me with yourself, and you can trust Me with those you love."

"You, too, shall have a tryst with your Master, but in My time."

Then help me to say, "OK, my Lord." But there are times when waiting is so hard, and understanding is harder, and even with trusting we need a great deal of help.

To know they are with the Master is our solace.

Yes, I know that it is theologically argued that man is a single whole, not two separable halves, body and soul. What he experiences here he experiences as a whole person, not one thing with the body and another thing with the soul. God has created us in wholeness, not two halves stuck together. But all this has to do with the here and now, as He has revealed it to us. It is part of this amazing combination that becomes one person by God's creative gift of life.

What God does about me and to me on the other side of this life, before the final resurrection, is something He has not described for us in any detail. It is His marvelous business. I cannot limit Him with my mind or my logic. I lean only on His promise.

This I know, that He has promised to take us to Himself, that where He is we may be also, and that is good enough. He said to the dying thief on the cross: "Today you shall be with Me in Paradise."

Let others discuss what exactly is meant by the word "Paradise." I'll live by, rest in, and hang on to the words *with Me.* That's all that really matters.

He also said: "I am the Resurrection and the Life; he who believes in Me, though he die, yet shall he live, and whoever lives and believes in Me shall never die" (John 11:25-26). He used the present tense when He said: "He who believes in the Son *has* eternal life." (John 3:36)

I have it now as His gift to the believer, and He has promised that *no one* can take me out of His hand, nor can they take out of His hand those whom I love and whom He has already called to Himself.

When you have seen a part of yourself move quietly away from this life, or if you have sat with someone who has had notice of shortened days, then it matters a lot to know that they slip away to beckoning arms and a waiting Master.

"Precious in the sight of the Lord is the death of His saints." (Ps. 116:15)

When along life's way He taps one of us on the shoulder, opens a gate by the side of the road, and says, "Come with Me to where your heart must long to be, from now on you shall be in My tender care," *it is a tryst with the Master!*

Then I can better endure the loss and the waiting, until I, too, can be along, shortly, for the great reunion.